Oscar Ilari

Learning Bridge is Easy

THE IMPORTANCE OF LEARNING THIS GAME, AND THE RELATIONSHIP IT HAS WITH IMPROVING THEIR QUALITY OF LIFE, A HELP FOR TEACHERS.

ScienciaScripts

Imprint

Any brand names and product names mentioned in this book are subject to trademark, brand or patent protection and are trademarks or registered trademarks of their respective holders. The use of brand names, product names, common names, trade names, product descriptions etc. even without a particular marking in this work is in no way to be construed to mean that such names may be regarded as unrestricted in respect of trademark and brand protection legislation and could thus be used by anyone.

Cover image: www.ingimage.com

This book is a translation from the original published under ISBN 978-613-9-07879-0.

Publisher:
Sciencia Scripts
is a trademark of
Dodo Books Indian Ocean Ltd. and OmniScriptum S.R.L publishing group

120 High Road, East Finchley, London, N2 9ED, United Kingdom
Str. Armeneasca 28/1, office 1, Chisinau MD-2012, Republic of Moldova, Europe

ISBN: 978-620-8-14527-9

Copyright © Oscar Ilari
Copyright © 2024 Dodo Books Indian Ocean Ltd. and OmniScriptum S.R.L publishing group

Content

FOREWORD 2
CHAPTER I- INTRODUCTION 4
CHAPTER II- OPENINGS 22
CHAPTER III. COMPETING AUCTIONS (OVERDECLARATION) 41
CHAPTER IV. VALUATION AND REVALUATION OF A HAND. 44
CHAPTER V. STRONG OPENINGS... 48
CHAPTER VI. CARTEO 53
EPILOG 55

FOREWORD

With this book, I intend to share experiences that I have gathered in 55 years of being accompanied by this incredible and exciting game that is bridge.

Now I realize that I enjoyed it in different ways. When I started it was a great challenge, but fortunately it did not supplant other activities that were more important: work, study. Besides, I played rugby in higher categories of this game, which trained me in several disciplines, fundamentally and in relation to bridge, the importance of playing as a team. For many years I was a coach of lower divisions, where, apart from the game, respect for the rival was taught and that after the game we shared a meal with those who had fought.

From this stage, a lesson I learned from some of the coaches I had was that we had to know how to lose, that we had to respect my teammate's mistakes, because I also made mistakes.

The reason for this explanation is that the game you are starting to play is tremendously competitive, and as you will never have a repeated hand in your life, that is to say, the same as one you have already played, everything is debatable.

But we add that in this game the one who makes the fewest mistakes wins, since we all make mistakes, and that in human beings is difficult to accept.

I think it is very important that they prepare themselves in this aspect, because if they do, they will be better players, and if they do, they will be better people.

Of course I was 20 years old there and today I am 78, so I'd better not go on with my story, because I would have to make several books of mistakes and successes.

But I continue with the subject of bridge, because when I retired I started teaching, and that is where I understood the infinite virtues that this game has, and that is what this book will be about, to help you enjoy it at whatever level you have, and to dispel the myth that it is impossible or very difficult to play it.

This will be the fundamental point that we will face, and I tell you that it is related to how to teach such a difficult sport with so many variables, you cannot add difficulties to it, you have to learn it in the simplest way.

This system that you are beginning to study is completely in that context.

And as I said at the beginning, I approach it with all the passion I have and with the firm certainty that I will help them.

I complete this part by promising you that I will not want to show you everything I know about bridge, but that I will put myself in your place, and I will give you all the time you need to understand what this game is all about. And fundamentally that they understand what it is about as quickly as possible, because in that way the game will fulfill the main function of activating their brain and that they incorporate into their life the possibility of practicing the application of logic. It will also fill hours of their day, for rest and entertainment, and to share with friends or other players in the world.

In this introduction I will talk about a topic of our near future: technological changes are having an exponential growth and modification, especially with artificial intelligence, very serious problems are coming for human beings. Since we will have to think and make decisions less and less, this will undoubtedly generate an atrophy of our brain. Incorporating elements to keep it active will be a necessity, and this game is a great solution.

I know it is something that has just begun, but the speed of progress will put humanity in a great challenge. Before, when I was a child, the telephone appeared, but the connection was through an operator, who had a console with many wires and connected you to talk; it took a long time for the telephone with direct dialing to appear and it took much longer for the cell phone and I don't tell you how the first ones were: it was a box that had a car battery and if you were lucky you could communicate with someone. After that everything started to be faster: smartphone, computer, more and more powerful and now artificial intelligence.

Therefore, I will try with this book to put you in the shortest time possible to play this game, but knowing the mechanics and how you should think in each of the instances of the game. The bridge is so wide and varied that applying this method will circumscribe you: in each stage the least amount of issues to be solved will be the least amount of issues to be solved.

I want to warn you that when I started playing in 1965 there were already great players. But they gave you some classes and then they gave you a little book, that, a few days after starting to read it, your head was a tangled bundle of wool, the concepts went anywhere without a fixed direction, it took you between 3 and 6 years to really understand the game. I will explain why this book can help a lot to understand it before.

CHAPTER I- INTRODUCTION

This book is to teach people who are starting from scratch, and also for those who already play no matter the level is good for everyone.

It is important that the basics are given in person by a family or friend, there are also many art and videos that teach the basics, when you already understand the mechanics of the game you can incorporate this book. Even this book if you follow it in a staggered way, that means if you take the topics one by one and until you understand it you do not pass to the second and so on, it will be very useful and will accelerate your learning.

The first thing we should prioritize is to have a partner or a group of people who play the same, since the most important thing is that my partner understands, with me, the distribution and the points I have. Here it is well established that this is a team game, since it is played with a partner and against another team formed by two players who will try to compete for who gets the most out of the cards they have.

This does not mean that we can't play with any other bridgist in the universe, we can do it and have fun just the same. Also understand each other even applying the concepts they are learning since the final result of the hand will be the best.

At this stage, what I do is to teach the system if it is in pairs, if not in four players.

There are players who want to learn on their own. I can give them a private lesson and once they have learned the basics, I can play one of the tournaments on the internet and then review the hands played and mark the mistakes made, learn about events that have just happened, which has a clearer effect on the players.

Returning then to play with my partner we must have a system, there are many and you can choose, the one you want, I recommend that this is as natural as possible because it offers fewer mistakes, within what is called natural system, there are many variants, I will give you guidelines, during this book, where and when the danger is and fundamentally and a stick, to help you define as many hands as possible. This in the auction

Normally we tend to want to play conventions and that is the worst mistake you can make, with three or four basic conventions of natural, you can cover 80% of the hands you will play in your life, also the most complex of bridge is in that 20% that remains to be learned, which will be introduced slowly, with the experience gathered, and you can play the level you decide and your time allows you.

I would like to add that one of the reasons why it is said that bridge is so difficult to learn is because the teachers, the experienced ones or, as in my case, those who know how to play bridge more or less well and start teaching, is that we do not have a studied and proven technique on how to teach. Today I can say that after many years I have experienced that teaching bridge in a staggered way is the most efficient. I teach openings from 13 to 20 and I stop on them until they master them and so on.

I always consider that teaching conventions at the beginning is counterproductive for new students, and what I do is to teach them openings, reply of the partner of the opener and second reply of the opener, within the basic principles of bridge. Because this is what is important because in this opening from 13 to 20 points are the most hands that they are going to play in their life. I clarify that it includes the 1st opening, but at the beginning of the teaching I advise not to use them until you have very well established the above and then spend a significant amount of time only to the 1st opening. Then I move on to a very basic competitive auction but that helps them to face any statement of the opponents, all based on showing points and knowing what scores have our hands, since the score depends on what level of play we can play.

The first is called partial which is played up to 25 points; then game, is played from 26 points; the next step is the slam for which 33 points are required and with 37 the highest game of bridge is declared the grand slam. This is well explained in chapter one where you have the fundamental bases to understand this game, but continuing with the score the couple must know what real score they have together, for this we must determine as accurately as possible the value of our hands and adjust to our level, if the opponents continue to intervene we pass. In this we have to be strict because it will depend on the final success. Another thing I want to tell you is that the bridge contract was created in 1925 in the United States by Harold Stirling Vanderbilt and he was the one who determined the necessary points to win in each of the heights of the game. This book has as a fundamental theme to know what real score we have to comply with this guideline.

The human being always wants to show that he knows a lot especially when he develops an activity that he shares with other people, and knowledge is not demonstrated by saying but by doing the right thing, and in this game if you are clear about the basics you will quickly solve the simple hands and you will have more time to find the solution of the more complex hands.

Of course, students are not all the same, it is in the teacher's ability to bring together those who learn faster so that they do not stop in their evolution and there are those who take longer, but the important thing is that they will also play and play very well with these teachings.

Within the topics of a system and according to each teacher, there are some that are more important, and determining what they are is what marks the spirit of the system. I give the greatest importance to think in points, and for this we have to learn very well what is called valorization and revaluation of a hand, and the second topic that I consider very important is the auction in competition, which for me is what makes a player grow faster and with a very solid base to finish off. On the first one there is a lot of bibliology that can be read, in this book the fundamental parts are briefly explained, what is different from everything is the backhand in competition and I consider it one of the fundamental tools of the system.

Note that I have always left aside the card dealing, since this important part of bridge is much more difficult to learn than the auction, here as it is only one of the players who manages the game, the final resolution of the hand will depend on him, that imposes a condition of the student which is the personal exercise and the time he dedicates to it, since the concept of counting cards, seeing which ones were played and knowing the distribution of the rivals is imposed. Everything is achieved with a lot of practice. As for the way to exercise, I advise you to enter a program and play only cards, that is the best way to remember the cards played and to repeat permanently the distributions of the hands. Playing the contra is much more difficult, because here again the pair acts, so you have to have information of other values and characteristics that do not include any of the learned ones. In this item I advise you to always mark the number of cards, there are more specifications in the carding title but always with few concepts to make things easier.

One of the pillars of this teaching is to ask ourselves **what did my partner say to me**, this question will help us to try to assemble the 26 cards that the side has. If the message is the right one, we will be able to know how many points we have between the two of us and which is the best contract, which can be a trump or a trump.

This is one of the most important sticks for players of any level, since for some reason those who devised the bridge contract started the opening with 13 points, and the reason is that if you have 13 points you are missing 27 points of the 40 and in the middle term those points are distributed equally among the other three players, that is 9 each one of them, and my side will have between 21 and 22 points (the sum of 13 for the opening and the 9 of the partner) this marks a supremacy of points over the rivals who will have 18 or 19, an indispensable requirement to not lose the level 1 of a contract. You who already know something about the game, know that the scores and distributions are variable in all the hands, I repeat with so much insistence this concept because it is undoubtedly the most important and the players do not get used to do it, that is to say, always think about the score of the hands.

The other important point of this book will be the one referring to the auction in competition, which I call the most important. This is because the opponent's intervention makes it more difficult to know how to combine our cards, and as I said, our whole system is based on knowing how many points we have honor-distribution. The development of this chapter keeps as all the book the simplification of what you have to learn, and you will realize when you learn it the differences that mark with other forms of teaching, but keeping everything important to get the desired result. I add that you can play this auction in competition with any player where there is a vsnyo that you can not do and I will mark it in the development of the chapter.

By now you will realize that this chapter sets many guidelines that will be indispensable for those who really want to learn and improve their bridge. I think it is good that people have different pretensions of knowledge, it is part of our life, that is why this book is useful for all players.

For this reason, and to avoid tensions, I say that I consider that bridge has to be a distraction, accompanied by social relations. When the classes are face to face I share other topics between hands, but when the auction begins and until the end of the carding I ask for maximum concentration, I also clarify that you can improve and have a level of play and the important thing is to have the ambition to keep improving it, that in life is fundamental because it imposes a challenge and that is what life is about, permanently creating new challenges.

Here a topic appears and it is that bridge is an Olympic sport and at the same time an intellectual activity as there must be few in the world, there is no doubt that creating challenges in daily life is not easy and even more to put them into practice. In the game we are playing there is a hand to play every 7 minutes, and as they are all different each one is a new challenge, but not only that but within the 7 minutes there are also challenges that add up, as a hand has the auction, the final contract, the carding if it is our turn and the defense otherwise, as each of them have different requirements, they produce challenges individually. This is what makes it so important for me surpassing other games of the so-called mind sports.

Relaxing I tell them that as you can play with a group of friends at home, or tournaments in clubs or tourist places, or also participate in international tournaments, this gives you the possibility of forming groups to meet, remember that I played bridge many years and it was an activity that left me many friends and over time we continue to see each other and play bridge. The hand ends and we usually discuss for a while, because it is part of the distraction. This mention is linked to a previous topic which is what the new generations will face.
where social life will be increasingly limited.

The myth they say about bridge, that it serves to protect against certain diseases of the head, may be true if we really learn to concentrate and think, and the fundamental difference is the level we want to achieve. But it is true that as the game is a pure application of logic, it can use sectors of the brain that are not easily developed.
Another issue is that human beings are competitive, and this game is very opinionated, the reason is that as there are millions of hands and none is the same, and there are millions of players, everyone can have a different opinion about the same hand. This explains why it is fundamental the partner and the understanding that the couple achieves. And this goes for all categories, since the super world champions, who play and practice 8 hours a day with the same partner and are professionals, go out of a tournament and discuss the hand.

You will say: Why do I play then, if it is so difficult and has such differences? To have fun and have a better quality of life, knowing that if I want to progress I can improve, studying and dedicating time to it. And that those discussions are the most fun of bridge when they are made between friends, to agree and say what I think without getting to the discussion with our usual partner is essential, there we have to talk to define how we understand that song or auction, because it improves the couple when we both know what we say or what we say. This is another contribution that the game makes for individual growth, a human being who has the ability to incorporate new things in his life is someone who will grow a lot, because in order to incorporate the most important thing is to learn to listen.

From the above comes a basic concept: as I make a mistake, the same thing can happen to my teammate, so I should not fight with him but talk hand in hand and have the intelligence that I could be the wrong one, and this will be what makes me grow as a player. This concept is born in all team games, I told you that I played rugby for a long time at a higher level, and I also coached teams, and one of the most important things I learned is to respect my teammate's mistake. I repeat this because this is useful not only in bridge, but in all our life relationships, friends, partner, work, etc..

At this point I will talk about something that is individual to each player and impacts on growth in the game. The human being is naturally an intuitive being, and in bridge we must be rational and logical, so let's breathe and review a second time the song or the play that we will do, this is another of the guidelines that we will see and set, at what time we should deepen. Notice that with the practice of these concepts we continue to learn lessons that go beyond the game and form human beings.

I went to a school of priests and they were teachers, some of them remarkable. One day the history teacher came in, with him not a fly could fly, and he said make groups of five and talk about communism, we got together and it was a deafening noise because we were all talking at the same time, after a few minutes he made us shut up and told us: I saw 20 people talking all at the same time, that is, they were thinking what they were going to say, no one heard anything, no one learned anything. It is essential to learn to listen, it depends on it how we get to the true value of our hands, it also provides us with data that later will be used both in the carding and in the counter.

I considered myself a good bridge player, and after teaching for 20 years, today I realize that every day I learn something new. Know, do not forget: each bridge hand leaves a new concept and reaffirms general guidelines of this game.

One of the many issues that the game has to banish, and it is also applicable to other activities, is to get stuck with the mistake of the previous hand we played. This is more common than you think, and causes disasters in the players. This topic seems minor but how many times in our life or work we have discussions or we made a mistake and we are several days to assimilate it. Know that all those days had stress and it is one of the worst evils for our life. Practicing it in the game will give us a practice to do it always. But be careful, when the moment is over we have to learn from the mistake we made to improve our game or our quality of life.

On the subject that bridge should be a programmatic subject in schools I have also had experience, but a negative one, since in several of the schools I attended and I had the support of the management, who informed all the parents of this possibility, the answer in 99% of the cases was that they did not want their children to learn to play cards and it was better for them to play a sport. I have no doubt that one or more sports are fundamental for the youth, but the lack of knowledge is very great since this game is the sport of the mind, apart from the innumerable ways in which as we have been seeing it contributes to improve the human quality.

But there were many people in the world who think it should be a subject in schools, and some who took on the project by even having a book made to learn, such as Bill
Gates in the USA, what they did was a book on bridge, but that book did not highlight the reasons why it is important to learn to play from an early age, they failed to highlight all the concepts that are poured in this book so that parents can make a decision with specific data on what bridge contributes to the education of their children.

Nowadays with the incorporation of computers we can play at home at any time of the day, it is very good, it facilitates the ways of playing and we can do it with greater ease and time. What we must avoid is to play automatically, because that works against us, because at times we act intuitively, and remember that I told you that this way of playing takes us back in our improvement and we lose the essence of the game, which is to think and reason.

Conclusion: the computer is good because we can play without having to leave our homes, but keep in mind what I said before.

I always have a duality of thought about this: is it very bad? Not so much if we know how to differentiate one situation from the other, when I use it as a distraction from when I play seriously, either in tournaments or at the computer or with friends, what I recommend is that we play bridge even if it is 4 hands but super concentrated, so that it is a dicipline and we get used to it. You will say but tea and dinner with friends are phenomenal, but I said that before I gave 30 m of class and there, all concentrated.

From what we have mentioned above, you will realize how many things we can practice with bridge that are useful for our daily life, as long as we are prepared.

We have been talking for a while and it seems very serious. So a distraction always comes in handy and I am going to take this opportunity to warn you about something that can happen. There is a special situation, which is when the married couple or life partners or close friends who live together play together, here you have to be very concentrated and apply a lot of logic. The duration of our marriage will depend on it, therefore I recommend that if a discussion starts, which is very common if it is about bridge, at some point one of them, whoever it is, say I propose to stop for 2 hours, relax and tomorrow we will continue.

I could go on and on listing principles, but I'll be mashing them together at each stage of the game, to give them more consistency.

From all that has been exposed so far, I want to make it very clear that this book has the mission of facilitating the learning of this game. But fundamentally, to emphasize each of the virtues mentioned, it is important in teaching to work intensely on the above mentioned, in order to incorporate them and improve in bridge and as human beings, not only in intelligence but also in life virtues.

Finally, I would like to inform you that this game has a set of rules, in which it is stated that any irregularities are punishable. This in my opinion completes the importance of playing bridge: whoever does not comply with these laws is punished as it should be in our society.

INITIATION

This chapter is for those who do not know the basics of Bridge.

1) WHAT DOES IT CONSIST OF?

The minimum number of players is four, playing in pairs.

The game is played with the French cards (the Poker cards) and they are all dealt among the four players, that is to say, thirteen cards for each player.

The game consists of two stages: REMOTE and CARTEO.

The Remate is the spoken part where the players express, by means of a special language, the cards they have in their hand and at the same time make a promise that they will have to fulfill in the Carteo.

The first call of the Remate is made by the player who dealt the cards, the DEALER. Then the turn continues to the left, and so on for the whole game, i.e. clockwise.

2) VALUE OF THE CARDS

The AS is the major, then the KING, then the QUEEN and then the VALET (or JACK); these are called honor cards.

Then the 10 continues and all the numbers follow decreasingly until reaching 2, which is the smallest.

There are four suits, which are the PIQUE, the CORAZÓN, the CARRO, and the TRÉBOL. The first two are called MAJOR, the following are called MINOR.

BAZA

A trick is the set of four cards formed by one card from each player, that is, if each player throws one card on the table, they formed a trick. This occurs during the Carteo.

Since each player has thirteen cards at the start of the game, the Draw will consist of thirteen tricks.

The initial card of each trick marks an obligation to continue the same suit; that is, if the player who starts a trick plays Heart, the other players must play Heart, and the player who plays the highest card is the winner of that trick.

Now as the game is a pair game, the trick will have been won by the players of the pair.

At the end of the Carteo, the tricks are counted, and according to the promise made during the auction, it will be determined if the promise has been fulfilled.

From this explanation we can see that the promise made in the auction is related to the tricks.

Let us order the concepts up to this point:

Deal 52 cards among 4 players, 13 to each player. The game is played 2 against 2.

First the Remate is performed, which is the spoken part of the game where the player tries to transmit the cards he/she has by means of a language.

At the end of the auction, a promise is made of tricks that one intends to win, in pair with his partner.

The Carteo is carried out and 13 tricks are played and at the end of the game the winnings of each side are counted and it is checked if the promise was fulfilled.

3)   TRIUMPH

We have said that there is an obligation to play the same suit (there is no obligation to raise or kill the card played) that has been sent in a trick; but this obligation cannot be fulfilled in the case of not having that suit (being FAIL) and in that case there will be the absolute freedom to discard any suit, or to fail.

During the auction, not only are tricks talked about, but also suits, and the side that makes the final promise is also in charge of choosing a suit as the main suit of the hand, and it is called the suit of TRIUMPH.

The usefulness of the same is that if one finds oneself at fault in a trick, one can play a card of another suit, and if the card is of the trump suit, one will win the trick even if the card is smaller than the others.

This possibility is only valid if one is Failed.

The more cards you have in the Trump suit, the more chances you have to win tricks. IF a Trick is going to be won by my partner and I have no cards of that suit, it will NOT be convenient to spend a trump.

Each trick is started by the winner of the previous trick, and the winner is free to start with any suit.

As we said in a previous paragraph, there are four suits: the PIQUE, the HEART, the CARRO and the TRUMP and any of them can be chosen as trump, but there is also the possibility of choosing to play No Trump, and in this case the trick will be won by the highest card of the suit that initiated the trick (there are no faults).

Example: If you start a trick (in No Trump) with a 4 of heart, and the other players play the 6 of clubs, the 5 of heart and the 8 of chariot; the trick is won by the 5 of heart.

4) BEGINNING OF THE AUCTION -- HIERARCHY OF THE CLUBS:

For the auction it is important to know that the clubs have different hierarchy and that the edges must have an increase with respect to the one that precedes them, so we will see that this increase may be in the number of tricks or in the hierarchy of the club.

The TRÉBOL is the smallest of the clubs, then follows the CARRO, then the CORAZÓN and then the PIQUE, and the greatest of all is the SIN TRIUNFO.

Let's see an example.

THIS	SUR	WEST	NORTH
1CARRO	1 PIQUE	STEP	1 NO WIN
2CARRO	3 TREBOLES	3 TROLLEY	4 TREBOLES
STEP	4 PIQUES	STEP	STEP
STEP			

This example is that of a complicated auction, where both sides have spoken and several trump options have been mentioned, with the last count being valid, i.e. 4 PIQUES, which means TEN TRICKS with PIQUE trump.

The player who dealt the cards (GIVER) is the first to start the auction and may, according to his cards, make a promise or say the word STEP, which means that he does not have enough values to speak.

The minimum number of tricks that a side can promise is seven, that is, a little more than half the number of tricks in play (thirteen) and that number of tricks is called ONE, that is, if one says ONE HEART, it means that he is promising SEVEN TRICKS (the minimum) and that he is choosing the heart as the trump suit.

The REMATCH does not have a stipulated limit of turns, but it concludes when, after having given everyone the opportunity to speak, there is a sequence of three consecutive Steps, which means that the same player cannot raise his own promise.

For convenience we will know the name used to name the players: NORTH - SOUTH - EAST - WEST.

Obviously NORTH and SOUTH will be partners and EAST - WEST their rivals. Example of an auction:

north east south west
1 clover pitch 2 clover pitch
Compi Step

NORTH has begun the chant by promising seven tricks and choosing the club of clubs as trump.

THIS announced that his hand is not fit to speak.
SUR Increased the pledge to eight tricks and kept the trump suit suggested by his partner.

OESTE also does not wish to speak.

Norte considers his partner's pledge adequate and decides not to increase it.

This continues to be silent and being the third consecutive step, the auction is terminated.

CONCLUSIONS:

The final contract is 2 TREBOLES, which means EIGHT BAZAS with Triunfo TRÉBOL. The side in charge of fulfilling the contract is NORTH - SOUTH.

Using the example, we will determine several words and names used in the Bridge language.

Norte, who was the first to name the club of Trébol, which remained as a trump, is directly in charge of fulfilling the contract, and is called DECLARANT.

SOUTH will be the DEAD and therefore will have to lay its cards on the table, in full view of everyone and they will be led by North.

EAST and WEST, who are the defenders, will try to prevent NORTH from winning their EIGHT BASES and to do so, they will try to win at least SIX.

5)   CARTEO

Once the Auction is finished, the Carteo begins.

The first card placed on the table is called EXIT, and this move must be made by one of the Defenders, and more precisely by the defender who plays before the Dead Man.

According to the previous example, the player who should make the Exit would be THIS.

Once ESTE has placed the starting card on the table, SUR, who is the Dead Man, proceeds to lower his cards and only at this moment are they seen.

Departure must be made before seeing the Dead.

After this, the carding begins and each side will try to achieve its objective throughout the thirteen tricks.

It is not essential to win the first tricks to achieve a better result, but the strategy is to make the best use of the cards to win as many tricks as possible. A NOVICE TRIES TO WIN AS MUCH AS HE CAN AND THEN ENDS UP LOSING IN THE LONG RUN.

The DECLARANT (enforcer) is SOUTH (FIRST TO MENTION THE POST) NORTH will be the DEAD.

WEST will be the one to go out (the one who throws the first card). Let's study the order of the auction:

EAST opened with 1 CARRO (7 tricks), SOUTH raised to 1 PIQUE (7 tricks but more hierarchical suit) NORTH raised to 1 SIN TRIUNFO (also 7 tricks) EAST had to raise to 2 to increase the auction with his CARRO suit and now SOUTH had to raise to 3 to name his TRÉBOL (9 tricks) and so the auction continued until SOUTH insisting with his PIQUE (he must have many cards for his insistence) took the CONTRATO.

At the end of the game, the result of the game will depend on whether it was completed and which trump suit was chosen.

6)   VALUE OF ASSETS

It is important to know that the value of the tricks is different, since they depend on the trump suit that dominated the hand.

Keep in mind that it does not matter with which suit the trick was won, but the suit chosen as trump. TRICK: 20 points for each trickMINOR KEATS

CART: 20 points each trick

HEART: 30 points per trick   MAJOR STICKS : 30 points per trick

NO TRIUMPH: 40 points the first one. 30 points each of the following.

Let's look at different examples of annotation:

2 TREBOLS (8 tricks) will score 40 points (2 x 20)

4 PIQUES (10 tricks) scores 120 points (4 x 30)

3 NO TRIUMPHS (9 tricks) is worth 100 points, which comes out of 40 for the first trick plus 30 and 30 for the second and third (40 + 30 + 30).

As we have seen, the score is taken into account on the tricks sung and the first six tricks are not counted, i.e. 8 tricks, in fact 2 are sung and 2 are scored.

In the case of taking extra tricks, these will be counted in the same way as the other tricks, i.e. if in the first contract of 2 TREBOLS (8 tricks) 9 tricks were won, 20 more points will be scored for the overtricks.

If, on the other hand, a contract is not fulfilled, a special value will be recorded for each minus trick taken, and each of these minus tricks will be called a penalty.

The value of these fines shall be uniform, regardless of the trump suit, and shall be scored in favor of the opposing side at the rate of 50 points for each trump trick taken.

Example: If we play 4 tricks (10 tricks) and win 8, it means that we have given 2 FINES and we must score 100 points (2 x 50) in the column in favor of our opponents, and those made are not worth anything because we did NOT comply.

The DECLARANT (enforcer) is SOUTH (FIRST TO MENTION THE POST) NORTH will be the

DEAD.

WEST will be the one to go out (the one who throws the first card). Let's study the order of the auction:

EAST opened with 1 CARRO (7 tricks), SOUTH raised to 1 PIQUE (7 tricks but more hierarchical suit) NORTH raised to 1 SIN TRIUNFO (also 7 tricks) EAST had to raise to 2 to increase the auction with his CARRO suit and now SOUTH had to raise to 3 to name his TRÉBOL (9 tricks) and so the auction continued until SOUTH insisting with his PIQUE (he must have many cards for his insistence) took the CONTRATO.

At the end of the game, the result of the game will depend on whether it was completed and which trump suit was chosen.

7)   CONTRACT VALUES

As we have seen, the first objective of this game is to win tricks, and above all, to fulfill the promise that was made in the auction and if we exceed the number of tricks fulfilled, the better, because we will score the plus as over tricks, but we still have to learn that another objective of the game is: The higher the contracts we play, the more important the prizes will be.

Therefore, the most convenient thing to do is to finish off as much as possible and for this it is important to know the different levels of the contracts:

BIG SLAM: Contract where all the tricks are promised (13).

SLAM or SMALL SLAM: A contract in which all but one of the tricks are promised (12).

GAME: Contract where the sum of the value of your tricks is at least 100 points. 5 TREBOLES 5 CARROTS (each trick is worth 20 points I need 5 tricks to reach 100 points and win the game) 4 HEARTS 4 PIQUES (each trick is worth 30 points with three tricks I don't reach 90 points with 4 I reach 120 points, game) 3 NO TRIUMPHS (here the first trick is worth 40 and the remaining tricks 30 each with three tricks I reach 100 points, game)

PARTIAL: Any contract that is less than GAME.

As can be seen, in the case of BIG SLAM or SLAM, the number of tricks is fixed regardless of the trump suit, while in GAME and PARTIAL, the number of tricks varies according to the trump.

PARTIAL CONTRACTSGAME SLAM G. SLAM

MINOR Sticks TRABOL and 4	TROLLEY1 - 2 3 and	5	6	7
MAJOR CLUBS HEART AND PIQUE 1 - 2 3		4y5	6	7
NO TRIUMPH 1 and	23-4y5 o	7		

When we learn to auction, we will look for the best contracts since if with our partner we decide to play in heart as trump and we think we can play a game, it will be convenient to sing 4 hearts and not 5 since both get the same prize (from Game) and 4 is one trick less than 5.

In the same way if we stay in a partial it will be better to play 1 or 2 and not go up to 3 since they will all be worth the same.

8) POINTS HONORS:

When we receive the cards we must value our hand and decide our song, whether we should speak, or say Step.

In order to facilitate the valuation of our hand, a value for the cards was invented more than half a century ago, taking into account the figures, which we said we will call honor cards.

He himself tells us:

the AS is worth FOUR points. The KING THREE points. The QUEEN TWO points. The JACK ONE point.

The idea behind this valuation is that the higher the score, the greater the presence of figures and the greater the chances of winning tricks.

As will be seen, if we add the values of the honors, we get that per club there are TEN points and therefore among the four players there are FORTY points.

Usually the Contract will be won by the couple that has more of these points, and for this we must learn the language of Remate.

Before going into language development we must know the association of honor points with contract levels.

How many of the 40 points do we need for these contracts? BIG SLAM: (13 BAZAS) we need at least 37 points. SMALL SLAM: (12 BAZAS) at least 33 points.

GAME: 5 clubs or corro (11 BAZAS) minimum 29 points. 4 hearts or piques (10 BAZAS) with at least 26. 3 no trumps (9 BAZAS) also with a minimum of 25.

PARTIAL: If we have less than 25 points, we must stop at the lowest contract, which is a partial.

All these scores are the sum of the two hands between partners and in order to know the score that our partner has, we must know the language of the auction.

For this reason it is of the utmost importance to be DISIPLINATE in the information provided, otherwise the only ones who are harmed is the partner, since the partner will make the wrong determination. The same as to determine the height of the auction that we can get to strictly conform to the points of the BANDO, and according to the table above mentioned

There is a point to develop that is the vulnerability, in tournament an element is used that are boards where the cards that will play in all the tables of the tournament come, and these have the information of who is a giver and how are the sides with respect to the vulnerability, and also maintains that order if we play with friends.

TABLE 1: north giver and the two couples are not vulnerable.

TABLE 2: East giver and now vulnerable is east-west and north-south non-vulnerable.
TABLE 3: south giver and north-south vulnerable and east-west non-vulnerable. TABLE 4:

west giver and both pairs vulnerable.

As you will see, bridge always gives the same possibilities to both sides since they are twice vulnerable and twice non-vulnerable.

The next four hands will have the same characteristics and so on for all the turns played. This is maintained in the friends game when cards are given to play without the use of slats.

This is a fundamental issue because both contracts and fines vary according to vulnerability.

I will now detail the tables of the additional points given by the contracts, i.e. how many additional points are added to the tricks won:

PARTIALS: 50 points are always added. E.g. I fulfill a contract of 3 tricks, i.e. I score 90 points (each of the tricks has a value of 30), to these 90 points are added the points for the partial and therefore become 140 points.

GAMES: Here we see the first difference between being vulnerable or not vulnerable. In the first cæ(i.e. vulnerable) we add 500 points to the amount of tricks won. E.g., I play 4 tricks is game and I add 120 points for the tricks won, to this I add the 500 points of prize and therefore I add 620 points. In the second case, i.e. not vulnerable, we add 300 or 420 points.

LITTLE SLAM: As to fulfill it, we must take 6 tricks that are equivalent to 120 points in the LESSER suit, plus 800 additional non-vulnerable points, that is, a total of 920 points. MAJOR GAME are 6 tricks for 30 gives 180, plus the prize which is 800 points, total 980 points, this is not vulnerable. Being vulnerable to the tricks taken we add 1250 points.

BIG SLAM: are in minor suit 7 bases. 0 is 140 and we add non-vulnerable 1300 points and vulnerable 2000 points.

ALSO THE FINES are different: if they are non-vulnerable a fine is worth 50 and vulnerable the fine is worth 100.

I will not go further into these issues because there are other differences, and explaining them all would be very complicated, and for this there is, for when they play, an element to use called BIDING-BOX, where it is on the back of each contract the corresponding points and also has a cardboard with an X that is the DOUBLE where are all the values of the fines that they give.

CHAPTER II- OPENINGS

Remember that I promised you that our system will be as natural as possible.

Everything that comes now to understand it well will depend on the knowledge already acquired and may be different. Remember that I promised you a very simple and natural bridge. All this development is based on scoring and distribution in the easiest possible way.

You take your 13 cards and count that you have between 13 and 20 points, if when it is your turn no player spoke, then our statement is called opening, that is, we open the auction. Be careful if before us a player has already said something, then everything we had prepared changes and we will move on to what is called a competing auction, that is, we will compete with our opponents for the final contract.

Coming back: if I have to open, we will think as follows:

OPENINGS 13 TO 20 POINTS (in order)

Openings   How to open

A)   15 to 17   balanced open 1ST

B)   Palo mayor 5th or   more-we open or ♥ ♠

C)   Diamond   4 open 1 ♦

D)   None of the above we   opened 1 ♣

E) 2 Weak (separate treatment) we open 2, 2 ♥ or 2 ♠ (6th pole and 2 honors)

The most important thing in the auction is to limit oneself to think only about the requirements of the moment of the auction in which we are.

E.g.: we receive the cards we sort and count that the hand has between 13-20 points and we think

A)   If we are balanced, balanced hands have only two impediments that transform them into unbalanced, that is to have a semi-fault or to have two dubletons. If so, it is no longer balanced and we move to the other point of the opening. So if I have 15 to 17 and it is balanced we say 1st and our partner knows that we have 15 to 17 with a balanced hand.

Here you will say this is very elementary, but what I am doing is teaching how this point works since everything is written in this way as if it were a multishop where one alternative eliminates the subsequent ones.

Eye - it causes some doubts hands that we have 18 to 20 points and are balanced, we doubt but do not open from 1st. So we move on to point B.

B)   If we have a major suit of 5 cards or more, we open in that suit, say a heart or a pique and our partner knows that we have between 13 and 20 points and the suit sung at least 5th , otherwise we move on to the next point.

C)   Notice if we have diamond 4 or longer and say a diamond, if we do not have any of the three previous ones.

D)   We say 1 club is called auxiliary suit since we can even have two cards.

As promised: read 10 lines and you have for the opening 80% of the hands you will play in your life.

PARTNER OF THE OPENER.

This point is when our partner opened and the opponents did not speak. Now we are in another alternative of the auction and the first thing we have to think about is if we have 6 or more points. If we don't, we pass. If we have 6 or more points then we pass to the replies on each of the openings.

Important: on the opening a) or 1st, we develop the answers in a separate chapter that follows the other answers, since the requirements are different from the ones we will mention now.

COMPANION RESPONSES TO THE OPENINGS B) Major stick 5th or more 1♠ and 1♥ :

DE 1

Here we will first talk about that the final contract can be a suit or a st, to be able to play with trump we need at least 8 cards. The explanation of why it must be 8 is that we have the majority of cards in that suit, the opponents only have 5 cards left.

1) **Support with 3 or more heart cards** we ♥ sing in the usual way

2   If we have **6 to 9 ♥ points**

3   If we have **10 to 12 ♥ points**

4   If we have **13 to 15 ♥ points**

Keep in mind that we say up to 15 points, because if our partner has a hand of 13 or 14 points with our 15 points he reaches 28 or 29 points and we are far from the Slam (33 points); and if he has 17 or more points he knows that our hands can reach Slam.

Then we will study a variable that allows us to better handle hands of more than 15 points, all in time, the purpose is not to confuse them. Here begins to work the importance of marking points.

If we do not have support for the opening stick, the following variables appear for each of the edges, always with the order of the openings and knowing that if we find one, we discard the rest.

2) **With 4 cards of ♠ or more we sing ♠** (always with more than 6 pts.) we say 1 pique. If we don't have it, we go to point 3.

3) **We sing 1st if we have 6 to 9 pts (with any distribution).**
Note: we can have an unbalanced hand, i.e. have 6 cards in a minor suit, but we still say 1st, this is because we prioritize showing our points, which are from 6 to 9 points, this helps our partner to know immediately how high in the contract we can play.

4) **We sing 2st if we have 10 to 12 pts** (with balanced hands) here if it **has** to be a balanced hand.

5) **We sing 3st if we have 13 to 15 pts** (with balanced hands).
If we have many points then something very important to play Slam appears which is how

many aces we have because if we lack 2 aces we cannot play Slam, and here appears one of the few conventions that we will play.

6) **We chant 4st to ask for aces** (this is the blakwood convention, ask for aces, and if the answer is "no ace" we chant 5♣, with 1 ace we chant 5♦, with 2 aces we chant 5♥ and with 3 aces we chant 5♠). You can also ask for "k" with "blackwood" but that we'll leave it for later, it usually doesn't help us with anything special.

4) **For songs at the level of two 10 points or more (the suit can be of four cards)**
Example: opening of 1♥, we answer 2♦ or 2♣ always with a minimum of 10 pts.

These chants have a very important condition, since the partner cannot pass and has to say something, here a figure appears in the finishing touches, which are **the forcing times**, that is, the partner has to say something obligatorily; **and the passable times** where the partner can pass. So when we say it is forcing or passable, we know what we are talking about. The reason is that as the opener has a minimum of 13 points and I have a minimum of 10 points, we add 23 points and the level of 2 cannot be lost and by the way a concept appears: who knows is the most important thing in the auction. Notice that from what we talked about so far we are passing information to our partner, in order to get to know how high the contract we can get and at which club we will play it, and everything is focused on playing a game, which is reached from 26 points.

Since the difference between a game and a partial is many points difference, I assume that you know how many award points each contract has. If you are not aware of this, I suggest that you go to any book you have from your previous education and reread it very well.

To summarize I say:
- Partial adds 50 points to the total of the bases.
- Game non-vulnerable 300 and vulnerable 500
- Slam 800 - 1200
- Grand slam 1500

I also warn you that one of the last topics we will touch on later is everything related to the importance of being vulnerable or not vulnerable and the alternatives it provides us with.

5) Chants in jumps of other suits, show 6 cards in the suit sung with honors and 13 or more points.

DE 1

1) **Support with 3 cards or more of pique** we sing ♠ (we see in what follows, that we must always have at least 6 points, both for the support of the suit as for the st) and here we develop with the usual order that if we find one of the variables discard all the others

2♠ **piques** if we have   **6 to 9 points**

3♠ **piques** if we have   **10 to 12** points

4♠ **picks** if we have from   **13 to 15 points**

2) We sing **1st** if we have   **6 to 9 points** (with any distribution)

3) We sing **2st** if we have   **10 to 12 points** (with balanced hand)

4) We sing **3st** if we have   **13 to 15** (with balanced hand)

5) We sing 2♦ or 2♣ with at least **four cards of those suits** and **10 or more points**.

6) We sing 2♥ with **5 cards** and at least **10 points**.

7) **We sing in jump of another suit**, if we have **6 cards** in the same suit, with good holding in honors and opening **13 points or more**.

I tell you that these two openings that we have talked about so far are the most important in an auction, because the natural system is based on finding 8 cards or more in a major suit, that is the most common contract, in fact the opening is called major suit 5, then you can call it sayac, or whatever you want, this is the basis of the natural.

Partner's answers to opening c) with 4 diamonds

DE 1 ♦

1) **Singing of a major stick at the level of 1: 6 or more pts** and the stick sung at least a quarter (1 ♠ or 1 ♥)

2) **Support 2** ♥ : **6 to 9 points** and ♥ at least **a quarter (4 cards from)** ♦

3) **1 st: 6 a 9** without the above and with any distribution.

But here we know that I have neither 4 hearts nor 4 pique, if I do, I am obliged to sing them.

2st: **10 to 12** balanced includes **four or more cards** from ♥ (5332)

(instead of saying 3 ♥ it is preferable to play **st** if the hands are balanced)

3st: **13 to 15** same as above.

4) **Jump song of another suit** shows **6 cards** in the same suit, with good holding in honors and opening of **13 points** or more.

Partner's responses to opening d)

DE 1 ♣

1) **Singing of a major suit at the level of 1: 6 or more pts** and the suit sung at least a quarter (1 ♠ or 1 ♥).

2) 1st **6 to 9 points** and any distribution

3) 2st **10 to 12 points** balanced distribution (includes 4 or 5 cards from ♣ or ♦)

4) 3st **13 to 15 points** balanced distribution (includes 4 or 5 cards from ♣ or ♦)

5) **Support** : **10 or more points** with **5 cards** in that suit (up to 17 or 18 pts. it is better to sing 2 clubs, but with only 10 pts. it is better to sing **2st**).

6) **Singing in a jump of another suit**, showing **6 cards** in the same suit, with good

holding in honors and opening **13 points** or more.

With this we finish all the alternatives that the partner of the opener has to inform his partner what he has in his 13 cards and he is passing him information of score and distribution, this way the auction is being built and that information is the one that is marking at what level the side can play and what suit it can play.

What follows is the second statement of the opener as long as the opponents have not entered the auction. Remember that any intervention by the opponent totally changes the meaning of the chants.

Here I stop to address those who want to teach or those who want to study with this book. I recommend that you practice what we have seen so far for several days to fix it safely.

The way to study it is: take a deck of cards, deal them, and of the four players, the one who has the opening makes it, without a competing auction, and the partner of the one who opened answers according to what has been taught. The object is to fix it in such a way that it is learned before moving on to another point.

Note that the continuation of the opening of 1 st is not yet here, that will be the next topic of study.

Among so many things to learn, you should know that this system is called natural, there are many variants, but in fact it should be called suit 5, because the objective is to find 8 cards in heart suit or pique to be able to play a suit.

To avoid cutting the first part of the bar tack, we will finish informing the hand with the stitch below.

SECOND OPENER'S DECLARATION (for opening of Palo)

This is another option, which has other requirements, which are given by the answer that the partner gave to his opening, then with the incorporation of the referred data there are two options: if the partner defined himself, e.g., he said 1 st which marks 6 to 9 points. In these cases, as the opener knows how many points the side has and what suit they will play, he will be the one to make the final decision of the contract.

In short, when we finish off there is always one of the two players that is described, in which case his partner will be the one who makes the final contract decision. But if the partner is not defined

then we have to mark how many points we have and in this case our partner will define the final contract.

A) When our partner was not defined

- if it sings a new stick at the height of one and scores 6 or more points and the sung stick at least fourth
- if he sings a new club at the height of two and scores a club tendentially 5th and 10 or more points.

And it is important when our partner says 1st, because on this point there are variables although it is already described.

As our opening goes from 13 to 20 we must mark how many points I have: Low zone goes from 13 to 16 points:

we make the lowest edge we can according to our distribution.

they can be 1st two of the suit sung by our partner and finally mark a second suit of lower rank than the one we sung first.

High zone 17 to 19 points:

we do the chant by skipping a level.

Which would be in leap, if you said a palo and we have a balanced hand we will say 2st (in the previous one we said 1st); if we have support to the sung palo I will say 3 of the same (before we said 2); and if we have a new palo now it can be of lower rank than the first one we sing or of higher rank we sing it in leap, all this marks our high zone.

With 20 points we sing game because if the requirement to talk about our partner is to have at least 6 points, with 20 we add 26 points and that is game.

See how our whole system is structured to score points and get used to thinking in points because this will be the stick to solve the finishing touches.

I was very repetitive because this is the heart of the system.

There is only one case in which you will not answer scoring and distribution, which is when you open from ♣ or ♦.

His partner answers 1 ♥, in this case if the opener has 4 cards of ♠ he must sing that suit at the level of 1 if he has an unbalanced hand of 13 to 15 points, and sings 2 ♠ if he has a hand of 16 to 19 and unbalanced hand .

We are in a part of the auction that you may consider the most complicated because we are getting to the definition of the contract, so I will try to simplify and not confuse with a lot of information that we can expand later towards the end.

Notice that in this variable, which occurs a lot, we have to say if we have 4 cards of pique 1 if we have 13 to 14 points and 2 if we have 17 or more. Here I stop because the logic of this game begins to appear. How many hole cards does the opener have? Only 4 because if he had 5 or more, he has to open from one of the suits and in this case he opened from another suit. Learning this is what will make the difference. **Besides, it is giving the guideline of the spirit of this system, which is above all to score points, because that easily shows us how high we can get in the auction.**

OPENING OF 1 WITHOUT A WIN (SUMMARY)

15 to 17 balanced

Remember that we had left this opening, which is included in the score from 13 to 20, pending.

If we have one of the options, the following are discarded. The most important is that when we are vulnerable against no, we have fifteen points, I advise not to open from 1 st if not from a minor, the concept changes in the position not vulnerable against yes, there always with 15 to 17 we must open from a 1 st.

When I told them that everything is prepared to protect them, this concept is fundamental, it will save them from many fines.

Why we separate this opening from the others from 1 to 8 p.m.

It is one of the most descriptive chants that exist in bridge, it marks two conditions 15 to 17 points and a balanced hand.

If I separate them, it is because the responses to this opening incorporate the conventions.

<u>What are they?</u>

Songs that what we say is not the stick we have but that ask us to say something or ask us something specific.

1)   Transfer

Here appears the second convention of the system. Why convention? Because the suit we declare is not the one we have, and we tell our partner which suit I have at least 5th is the next in rank.

We are going to play tranfer to the four posts because in this way we simplify the finishing and we have less chance of making mistakes.

The purpose of the transfer is because it is always in st's hand that the opener should carry, because it has the greatest strength and should receive the output.

In these cases the only requirement to do so is to have:

5 cards or more of major suit and zero to + points (i.e. regardless of the score) AND have **6 cards or more of minor suit** to transfer to minor suit.

Why such a difference? for minor suit we have to play at the level of 3 and with few points it is very dangerous. When we make the transfer, the partner has the obligation to say the suit that we ask him to say, it is not convenient to take any transgression to this request.

1a) Transfer to the main pole   if we say 2 ♦ we ask you to say 2 ♥

If we say   2 we ask you to say 2 ♠

1b) Transfer to minor stick   if we say   2 we ask you to say 3 ♣

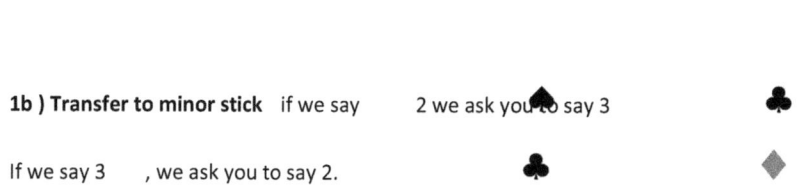

If we say 3   , we ask you to say 2.

2) With less than 9 points

We say **step** .

When they are masters they will invite with 8 points, but that is for great card players. The reason is that even with 17 points from the opener the total score is 25, which is not enough to play game, here we see two of the things I talked about at the beginning that I consider fundamental: the points to play game and how the system protects players with less experience.

3) if we have 9 points or more 3a) steyman

Here is the third convention of our system, I already told you that convention is when we sing a suit that we do not have and it has two functions: either to mention the suit that I ask him to transfer or to ask him something 2 clubs, steyman asks which major suit 4 you have.

Here there is an important point, many open from 1 st with 5to major suits, I recommend to open from 1 in suit. Reasons: we fulfill faster the objective of finding 8 cards in major suit and if I have 15 or 16 bad cards I treat it as a minimum hand; and if I have 16 good or 17 I treat it as a strong hand.

The requirement to do so is to have one of the two majors with at least **4 cards and 9 or more points.**

This is done by saying **2 ♣**

"Do you have any four-card major suit(♣s)?"
The answers are:

     2♣ if it has 4 cards or more and does not exclude the ♠

2♠ if it has 4 cards or more and does exclude the ♥

2♦ if none of the above.

3b) play st

If we have **9 or more** and **no major clubs**, we will play st and say:

    2 st   without have   **9 to-10** points

    3 st   with   **11-12-13-14-15** points

    4 st   (quantitative)   **16-17** to play 6 st

    6 st   **18 19**

5 st   (quantitative) **20-21** to play 7 st

7   st22 onwards in this case, it is convenient to go through 4 st because an ace may be missing

4)   *hands that we have more than 13 points and a 6th or longer stick.*

We sing that stick in jumping Example:

<u>Opener</u>   <u>partner</u>

1st   3♦ or 3♥ or 3♣ shows 6 cards and slam claim, the only suit that we can not sing is ♣ because this song was left for the transfer to ♦. All chants in a system have to have a justification that favors to reach the best contract, and first set a suit of play, with the caveat that partner says 3 st, now any other suit you mention tells you that you are interested in the hand and goes in search of playing 6. How a search for slam follows by way of cui-bid we will discuss in the next book, I always tell you learn the simple for when you have experience begin to incorporate complex issues, so if we want to investigate 6 we go through 4st.

Example: <u>a k xxxxx a q j 10 xxx a q xxxxx a j 10 9xxx</u>

Continuation of the auction according to the answers

To better identify the position is the partner of the one who opened 1st.

- **About tranfer**

We will see only the transfer to major clubs since on minor clubs we will do it only to pass. This is very important because if I have a 5 or 6 with a score of 10 or more I say 3st and if I have a minor 6 with more strength I call the jump. Here appears a very important caveat, if the good long suit is a diamond I say 3 diamonds, if the suit is a club I have to say 4 clubs, since 3 clubs is a transfer to diamond.

Note

Those who play more complicated use the edges of 4 clubs and 4 diamonds, to be able to play heart or pique, it is stupid because the system has the transfer and the same card the player who opened from 1 st. This is one of the many reasons that using so many conventions is generally unproductive and serves to confuse.

Example 1

Aperture 1   stresponse 2♦

2nd answer opener   2pass with one hand up to 8 stitches

3♥   (from **9 to 10 points** and ♥ **at least 6th**)

2 -3♠♣ or 3♦ virtual forcing game , we ask the partner if he has honors or cards of that suit to play game or if he has the maximum of the st (17 points) gives the opportunity to choose the best contract.

2st with 9-10 points and balanced hand (5332) invites

3st with 11 or more points and balanced hand (optional).

In both cases the **1st** opener will decide on what is best to play.

If after the transfer we make a jumping chant another slam force stick.

3♠ (in this case stick **5th** and the ♥ **5th**)

4♣ or 4♦ (clubs at least **5th** hand with slam possibilities.

Example 2

Yes we have   5♠ and 5game ♥ strength

opening   1answer   2transfer ♥
2nd answer opener 2♠ 2nd answer 4♥
(shows 5 and 5 in both suits) is to play game in one of the two suits, if the opener of 1st has

both third suits he chooses ♠ to play the hand himself.

Example 3

handling of minor bicolors

Opening **1st**   answers 3 ♥ canto forcing

3 st   4   (sample of at least 5 and 5 in the two game ♣♣ in any of these clubs)

3if it has the single color 6th pass or it says 4 ♦
diamonds

- **About steyman**

    According to the answer and the number of points we have, we invite or go to game

- 2♣ 2♦ we will say **2st** with **9-10 3st** with **11+**

- 2♣ 2♥ or 2♠ if it is our suit we will say 3 inviting 9-10 points. If we have 11
at 14 we say 4 of the suit sung. If it does not coincide with our suit we say **2st** with 9-10 and
3st with 11+

Here again there is a reason why it is a game that allows you to apply logic. If we say 2 hearts and our partner says 2 or 3 no trumps, and we have the quarter spade, we will now play spade because steyman is made with a quarter major suit and if it is not the one that sings or is heart, it is certain that he has 4 cards of spade.

At this moment I take the opportunity to make a reflexión that can help you a lot in this game. When I say and explain all this and talk about applying logic you automatically answer it is obvious, how can I not know, but I advise you to practice the application of these concepts and before answering automatically, stop to think about what my partner's chant means. Players **think that if they play fast they are better players and it is exactly the opposite.**

In case we have slam strength we will go through **4st** (which is the aces question), but in this case we will sing directly **4 st** which is a quantitative chant:

1st and the answer is directly **4st**

Statement with minor bicolor

If we have 5 and 4 in minor clubs and game strength we always finish off **3st** (even if it is 5-4-3-1).

With probable or certain slam strength and distribution of at least 5 and 5 we finish off with

1st   3♦

3st   4♣ (we ask our partner to choose between 5♣ and 4♦ (this chant allows us to consult aces with **4st**)

Intervention on the opening of our 1 st O is a competing auction

I include this one here so that everything related to st is clearer. I tell you: a teacher went to play with one of the best players in the world and when he asked him what we play about intervention to 1st; the great player replied: I will send you later the 300 pages I wrote about this. Moral: it is one of the most debatable topics in bridge, so we try to simplify it as much as possible using the natural.

A)   if the opponent **doubles** (i.e. has another **st**)

a1) if we have **6 ,7 or more** points **we pass**

a2) if we have **few points** we redouble (it is a call for help and our partner must sing his best stick, even if it is fourth.

a3) if we are in a position of **"we are vulnerable"** and **"they are not"**, and we have **9 points or more**, we use all the conventions of the **1st-opening** (keep in mind that the force is behind our partner, so we should have a better hand than when there is no data).

a4) if **they are vulnerable and we are not**, or we are with equal vulnerability we pass to the **double**

B)   if they intervene with a **stick chirp**

b2) if we sing a stick, it is **5th** with some honor and strength up to **8 points**

b3) if we say **st, 2st from 6 to 8 points and ataje al palo cantado, with 9 or more we say 3st**

b4) if we **double it is penalty**

b5) 3♣ en steyman

b6) if we have a game strength and a **5th major suit** we sing it in jump if we do not pass the 3 st level, otherwise we go through steyman.

Intervention on the opening of 1st by our opponents

Here it is important in which position was the opening of our opponents, if it is to our right or if we are behind him, our score is worth more and with 15 we can double; but if the opponent's opening is to our left, if we are going to double we must have 17 points, I advise that if we do not have 17 points we can sing a 5th stick, if we do not pass.

The other option is according to the vulnerability to declare a 5th pole.

Note: there are several conventions to show bicolors, I do not recommend them because it is difficult to handle for inexperienced players, of course if they are stable couples and want to use them and study them deeply, they can in some cases be useful.

I insist once again that this corresponds to the competing auction, a subject that will be discussed in more detail in the next chapter.

Recreation

Here I take a break from information and remember the things that at the beginning could not be well understood and as we move forward are at least more understandable.

I talked about the system being fundamentally natural, as you make fewer mistakes, than when you play a lot of conventions.

I said that it was a system based on counting points, since there is a reason for the existence of game levels and the points needed to play those levels.

I talked about it being in two stages of the game, finishing and defense, a game of teammates because if you don't know what your teammate scores you can't succeed.

And I also said it was created for all levels of players.

SUMMARY OPENING 2 WEAK

It opens with 2 of a 6th suit and with two major honors in that suit (both are indispensable requirements), in all suits except clubs.

That is in 2♠, 2♥ and 2♦ Score 9 to 12

Impediments: 1) if we have a quarter major suit (of a suit other than the opening suit)

2)   if we have two aces

Response from the opener's partner

A)   **Without intervention of the op.**

1)   with support cards to the partner's suit and not many points up to 10, sing the support according to the vulnerability, if it is "not" against (**not vulnerable**) you can sing very high, if it is **vulnerable** you have to be very careful. It is also important the suit of the opening because if

is ♥ or ♠ should be increased. These edges are not similar to those of one's openings.

2)   with support or possibility of game (you have to think that you have no opening, therefore to look for game you must have more points) we say **2st**. This canto asks opener if his hand is good or weak (knowing that he has no opening).

2nd response from the opener

A)   if your hand is minimal repeat the opening stick Example: opener partner

2♥ 2st

3♥ (you are replying to the partner who has a minimum hand)

B)   if your hand is good name another suit where you have honors or 4 cards or more

Opener   partner

2♥   2st

3♣ or 3♦   (you are showing a good hand with honor on the sung stick)

4♣ or 4♦ (it is showing you 6   **and 5** on the sung stick)

The punch line is always handled by the opener's partner (the 2 weak opener cannot speak again).

The opener can only speak if the partner tells him 2st Any other stick sung by the partner is passable.

> If the partner passes and the counter intervenes, the opener cannot speak again.

B) **with the intervention of the adversaries**

A)   The **2st** keep asking the question, "**what does the opener's hand look like**?"
B)   The double is a penalty
C)   Any other song is passable

Here I am going to introduce the so-called prohibitive opening, since the two weak is one of them.

But the vast majority believe that the prohibitive ones are the opening of 3, 4 or more and I am going to refer to them.

Repetitive but important: I will explain them in a very simple way.

These openings are made by losers and are directly related to the level of that opening.

What we say is that we have:

A)   If we are not vulnerable we are down 3 ridge bases realized
B)   If we are vulnerable we are 2 below the realized edge

Everyone thinks that just because I have 7 cards of one suit, I have a prohibitive card, but it is when those 7 cards have included

Ex. a-k-k-q-j-xxx these are to make seven bases

With this I will say 4 of the stick if I am not vulnerable. And 3 of the stick if I am vulnerable.

A lot for having site cards but with few honors makes a prohibitive and does not correspond.

What is it good for? The partner will see with his honors how many of these losers he can cover. And that way he will be able to know how high he can go in the auction.

In general, they are more useful when the player is not vulnerable, since they obstruct the rivals' shots and the partner can make a preemptive call, since it is convenient for the side not to fulfill the contract, even if the contract is doubled, because it improves the score if the rivals have a game.

This is the essential of the prohibitive and it is in simple form what you have to know, and I repeat you have to adjust to the system that we are playing, not to pass wrong information to the partner because of that the errors appear with which we lose the games that we are playing.

E.g. many people with a holding of a-q.-10-9-xxx count it as if they made 7 basas and it is far from being so, to count 7 losers with this holding it is necessary to add any other card, that is to say to have 8 cards of that suit.

All this explained so tersely seems to be more difficult to understand, the players are used to have 10 or 15 sheets of paper on each topic we touch, because they are explained a thousand variants to solve these issues, I believe that knowing the essentials and having the spirit of what is important, we know how to solve problems with few things.

In addition, this allows the player to grow because they have to reason and grow in the game, with the experience that each hand they play gives them.

And this is fundamental because, as we said at the beginning, bridge can have an unimaginable number of hands (40 million or more) and making a book that explains that number of variables is irrational because of its impossibility.

This book is written with basic teachings that allow you to solve a very important amount of the hands you will play, and will allow you to think faster because you will know the essential and most important issues to solve them.

CHAPTER III. COMPETING AUCTIONS (OVERDECLARATION)

Here we begin what is for me the most important and best resolved chapter of the book, of course always perfectible and open to opinion. We will divide it into two parts.

a.   When we open and the rivals interfere.
b.   When they open and we overdeclare.

Notice that it is within the tonic of making it simple, like the whole book. I also tell you that this can be, depending on how you teach something of three or four pages or more. To enclose in only two alternatives something that has millions of possibilities is already an achievement. But I tell you that even if it seems very simple in practice you will see how fast the hands resolve and obstruct the opponent's shot.

In this chapter is where the concept that I would like you to incorporate in your bridge is best exposed, which is the description of the hand and fundamentally the sum of points that we have between us to know at what height of the auction we can play.

A) We open from either side and the opponents enter the auction, that is to say, a competitive auction is initiated. They have two alternatives:

1) can sing a stick

With this variable, we can intervene and the information we give to our partner is determined by the points we have.

At this point we will talk about a fundamental issue which is vulnerability, because in case of being vulnerable our intervention must be more solid and not vulnerable we can enter with less points. The other issue to consider is if our singing is at the level of one we can speak with fewer points, but the higher the level, the stronger we can speak.

A) if we sing a stick that is not that of our partner or the rivals we score from 5 to 8 points and the sung stick at least 5th with some honor, in case of not vulnerable that would be the score ,on the other hand if we are vulnerable already instead of 5 we should have

b)   with 9 points or more we double
c)   if we pass we have nothing

d) if we have support to our partner's stick, we will inform him/her in the usual way: height of 2 from 6 to 9; height of 3 10 or 11; height of 4 13 or 14 (this edge always on bigger sticks).

I want to remind you that our system marks points, but this variable changes a little bit from what is natural, since in this system if we say that a club is 10 points or more, it leaves the hand very open and without knowing at what real level we are, it is convenient to be able to intervene even with few points, since today bridge is more aggressive and the opponents sometimes enter the auction with few points. We always have to know how many points we have, to know up to what level of auction we can reach and let them say what they want.

Note that with these songs our partner according to his score knows up to what level we can intervene, if we sing a stick and he has between 13 or 14 points he knows that we can not go beyond the level of 2. On the other hand, if we say that we have 9 or more points, he tells us that he has the lowest hand and we know that he has between 13 and 14 points, on the other hand, if he sings in salo or makes cui-bid we know that he has the high zone 18 or 19 points. I repeat this variable because it is the most important one, it can happen that our partner opens from a higher suit if we have support we will sing it according to what is combined in the system, and if the intervention is higher than the level that we can support we will pass.

Point 2 the rivals enter with double, the edge of any level suit marks a suit tendentially 5th and with some honor and from 5 to 8 points. In other words, we repeat the formula of the previous intervention. The best thing about this alternative is that we keep the same concept for both cases, our side always knows at what level it is, this is similar to the natural that everyone plays, since talking about a doblo marks weakness.

Of course if we redouble we have 9 or more points and each one of the partners will describe himself, with songs of weakness, doing inversion or jumps with more strength, all the songs in this stage are natural.

Point 2, they open and we intervene in the auction.

A) Intervention with a stick, this must be 5th and have honors and the score ranges according to vulnerability between 9 to 13 points.

But if the hand has between 12 and 14 points we can sing a very good 4th suit since we should not pass with that score.

It is also very useful because it marks a good exit if it corresponds to our partner. Therefore we must know that the sung stick can be fourth.

The risks are lower because it is almost impossible for us to play a game, the counter opened and we also have an opening, there are 12 or 13 points left to distribute, it is difficult for them not to be divided.

B) If we intervene with doblo we mark a hand with 15 or more points, we can do it with 14 if it is a good hand, this edge is very important for several reasons.

The main one is that if my partner has 9 or more points he has a high possibility of playing game, and he has to indicate it to me with an important chant or with a ciuibid (chanting the opening suit of our opponents). This puts us in a game situation.

If you have fewer stitches, make the lowest possible edge.

The other issue that allows us to protect ourselves from the possibility that with 15 or 17 points, if we have ataje to the opening and balanced hand, the natural thing to do is to say 1 st and we run the risk that the player who follows has all the missing points and doubles the contract, since this possibility, that of saying 1 st, we will always have, since with the double the auction remains open and we will be able to talk again.

This folding edge includes longer sticks and any distribution since, as I said before, we will always get the finish again.

And the only case that can not reach us is if our partner passes, that is to say, penalizes the opponent's opening because he has many cards of that suit and has the peace of mind that we have 15 points or more.

As you will see there are many advantages of this edge and it surpasses by far the natural doblo edge, in the natural one that can be made with up to 12 points, which means that our partner never knows what is happening, and the rivals have the advantage that if they have all the opposite points they can penalize us very easily.

CHAPTER IV. VALUATION AND REVALUATION OF A HAND.

For me this is the second most important issue as it gives us the true score of the hand and how we play points.

Keep in mind that to revalue a hand is to add to the natural points to k q j, points for other reasons, and a hand that has 10 honor points can be transformed into 12 or more points if the valuation is positive.

But we also have negative revaluations, in which case a hand that has 10 points must be considered 8 or less.

A)   hands that play with triumph

B)   hands playing no trump

For the first hands that we will play trump, the points must be added once the team knows that we will play with a trump suit, and very important, never value a hand until we know exactly what we will play with a chosen trump. I will indicate the most important issues to keep in mind:

1)   have more wins than the 8 required and we add the first win plus 2 additional points and the remaining 1 more.

That is, 8 are required to play trump but we can have 9 or more and they give additional points.

E.g. my partner opens from 1 heart and we have 4 hearts in our hand, there we already know that we have a total of 9 hearts and that additional trump adds 2 points to my hand.

My partner opens from 1 heart and we have 3 support cards, here we can't add anything but we know that we will play trump.

2)   another way to add points to a hand is to have 1 card (semi flop) in a suit other than trump, there we count 2 additional points, only if that card is a j or a q we cannot count the value of that card.

In the case of having 2 cards (doubleton) we add 1 additional point, here also if within the 2 cards are the a or the k, we also add 1 point, but if we have the q or the j we cannot add points for having 2 cards.

3) there are other issues to add score to the hand, if the same are constituted with a and k can have a better valuation, you can add a (plus), which means that when we have these values we can if we have doubts about the final contract are a determinant to add them and play game or something else.

Hands that have a k in the same suit are much more important, in these cases 1 point per distribution can be added for this reason.

4) We have said many times that in bridge the partners must describe what they mean, because e.g. showing a second long suit is useful to our partner if he has cards or honors in that 2 suit, they achieve what is called double fit, that is two long suits with good honors. This assures that by the sums of cards that we have in those two suits we can count, adding them together, the number of winning trumps. For example, we have in trump 5 trumps and my partner has 5 clubs where we both have cards and honors, this almost certainly gives us that we will win at least 10 trumps.

Because of the importance of this information, it is necessary to make constructive edges. And you have to avoid kangaroo edges, so as not to take space away from the partner and to be able to provide more information. The meaning of what I am telling you in this point is that if my partner shows me a second long stick that he has in his hand, and I have honors in that second stick, our hands have plus values to take into account. And an additional point should be added for distribution.

The clearest example is our partner opens from 1 piq and we have support and 10 points or more, but in addition we have 5 clubs cards with some honors.

Because of the score we could directly say 4 piq or game, but it is convenient to say 2 clubs to pass this information. Besides, this chant is what is called forcing, that is, our partner has the obligation to say something and after the partner speaks, now we chant 4 piq, then our partner learns that we have 5 cards of clubs and support to piq, and he would have the possibility to revalue the hand and under certain requirements to reach a slam.

Here appeared a denomination in our bridgistic lexicon, the term "forcing", which I will explain in more detail at the end of this title.

5) Another issue that is used to apply what we are learning is if we have information from our rivals. If they don't make any chant this doesn't change anything, but if any of them intervened in the auction that helps us a lot in the revaluation and valuation of our hand.

A) if the opponent to the right of us opened, our hand if it has a score we have to give it much more value than it really has.

The reason is that if we have k and q, which are uncertain values, in that case there is the greatest possibility that we can do those honors.

On the contrary, if the opener is to our left and we are in front of him, our hand will have a negative score because the honors we have are less likely to be converted into basas.

B) if our partner opened his hand and the next opponent calls a club and we have a k or q behind him, that honor becomes more valuable because we can surely do it.

C) On this subject of information, there is one that is not very widespread and is given many times.

Ex. The giver opens with 1 heart, my partner says 1 piq or he has 5 or more cards, the next one says 4 hearts and we have 3 or four heart cards and few honors, but we have support or 3 or more piq cards, the information we receive is that as the opponents have 8, 9 or more hearts, we now know that our partner has 1 or none, so with few points we can say 4 piq. This is an example to understand what it means to use the information.

Regarding point 2, that is, when we play ST: The elements to revalue the hands are less because to play game to ST it is necessary to add the necessary points for game, slam or grand slam, therefore, only if we have long suits, that is, 5 cards or more, and always if they are minor, either in the opening or in the response, we can add 1 or 2 points to the total (with the majors we must play that suit, either game or partial). From the above, my partner opens with 1 st and we have a suit 5 or 6, we will add points for each additional card.

An example that explains the concept well is if our partner opens from 1 st and we have a club 6th of clubs or diamond made up with two major honors, A and Q sixths, with only 6 points we must say 3 st.

The other issue that can improve our hand is if our partner opens from 1st, the counter intervenes with a club and we have e.g. K J x our hand has one more point of value .

I also told them that I would show them how to learn to use the logic that this game has, and this whole chapter is pure practice of logic, as information is applied to improve or worsen a hand.

I take this moment to remind you that vulnerability is one of the most important factors in this game, and I told you that when we are vulnerable we have to be more careful to get into the auctions than when we are not vulnerable, there you can put in jumping sticks to obstruct the understanding of our rivals.

And all these issues vary in each of the hands (know that it is impossible that in all the years you play you can be given a hand that you have already played) so being very attentive and use all these logical resources according to the state of the hand, makes this game a creation, ability, concentration and logic that has no other card game or other diciplines.

At the beginning I told you that, given the exponential changes that the world will undergo in a few years, having a tool that keeps us with an active and thinking brain will be of vital importance. The other thing I promised you is that this book eradicates the belief that bridge is so complex, we are almost at the end of the book and I don't think that everything explained by the simplicity with which we saw it has so many difficulties. The reason for the summary of the points we saw is so that our brain can develop by applying few concepts that allow us to cover as many hands as possible.

CHAPTER V. STRONG OPENINGS

Two without triumph

Balanced hands with 21 or 22 points

With balanced hands without 5to major clubs (these should be opened with 21p of 1♠ or 1♥, and with 22 p of 2)♣

The answers to this opening are the same as in 1st, but the score is modified and with 4 points we play game that we will choose in major suit sing 3♣ steyman or trasfer, or in st according to the characteristics of the hand.

Here the possibility of playing small slam is increased, since with 11 points or more we know that we are in 33 p. It is possible to play in minor suit or in major suit - we have the necessary elements since we use the steyman with 3 clubs or transfer them to major suit only. If we have minor suits without slam we sing 3 st unless the minor suit is 6th or longer, in which case we always transfer to the four suits.

If we have minor fourths or fifths with slam pretensions we will use a slam search convention with minor clubs over a 2-st opening that I develop separately.

Opening of two clovers

This opening is the strongest in the system and when we make it, the side cannot stop until it reaches the game.

The most important requirement to make it is to have between 3 and 4 losers (it is difficult for beginners to determine losers); another important requirement is to have several defensive bases that are aces and kings (this means that a hand with a great two-color cannot be opened from 2♣, since no one guarantees that the honors we have in that two-color can become defensive bases.

To help in the first part of learning when we have more than 21 points and an unbalanced hand we will open from 2♣ (that way we cover all possible openings).

Responses

Negative: 2♥ is made with less than 8 points Positive: 22♠ 2st 3♣ or 3♦ are positive edges Conditions:

With 7 points if these are an a and a k

With 9 points or more, if there is at least one k With 8 points or more, if there is at least one a Continuation of the auction on the answer of 2♦ 2st mark 23 or 24 points and balanced hand

3st mark 25 or 26 points balanced hand

Any sung club is essentially a 5th club or longer with unbalanced distribution, remember that the partner cannot pass until he reaches the game.

There are special situations in which we can pass before reaching the game:

1) when responder after giving the refusal of 2♦ ,and before any chant from opener, responder sings 2st, it is used to warn opener that he is very weak, 1 or 2 points only. In case of having more points it is advisable to sing a new suit even if it is 4to avoiding 2 st.

2) with negative response of 2d and opener says 2st in this case shows 23 or 24 balanced points, responder with 0 point does not reach 26 minimum required to play game, so it passes.

Another important issue is opening 2t response 2d (negative) opener says 2c or 2p for sure fifth suits, responder within his weakness if he says 3 of the same suit is stronger than if he says 4 of that suit (within his weakness appears here the revaluation of the hand). Another very important issue is that if the partner of the 2t opener is positive the suit called is not necessarily fifth because there are variables of unbalanced hands. With fourth suits e.g. a 4-4-4-1 tricolor. Another alternative to sing suit 4to, is if we have an unbalanced hand but the suit 5to is without any honor and in the suit 4to has the honors, here it is preferable to sing the suit 4to.

As long as the hand Is balanced we sIng 2st as posItIve, even If we do not have three-pole attacks I can have akqx-xxx-xxx-xxx-xxx-xxx- and I say 2st.

With an opponent's intervention the double is always a penalty of either partner, if after the intervention it is up to the partner of the opener to speak any stick I say (which can be 4th) is positive, pass is negative as if I had said 2d.

Remember that the 2t opening is a forcing game, so you must go slowly and describe yourself, it is not necessary to make jumps to mark long suits. Only if the opener does it and that is imposition of suit, you want to inform that the contract will be played in that suit even if partner fails.

A necessary element with strong openings that have a greater chance of playing slam is to know how many aces we have, and this convention is used for that purpose:

Roman keycard blackwood (rkcb)

Mr. Easley Blackwood developed the Blackwood convention so that slam could be auctioned only when in a position to do so. His convention has been modified and has generated many variations since it came into use.

One of these variations is called **roman key card blackwood.**

The rkcb is used only after you and your partner have agreed on the trump suit. The auction must have confirmed support for a suit or one of the players in the pair showed enough length in a suit for both to accept it as trump before the 4nt chant is assumed to be rkcb.

This is one of the most difficult aspects of rkcb, so it is important for the partner to be clear about when a club becomes a trump.

If you have agreed that a certain suit is trump, the answers to 4nt give information about 5 aces, the 4 aces plus the k of the trump suit.

The meaning of the answers to 4nt is:

- **5♣** 0 or 3 key cards

- **5♦** 1 or 4 key cards
- **5♥** -- 2 key cards, without the q of trump

- **5♠** -- 2 key cards with the q of trump

- **5nt** -- 2 or 4 key cards and a useful bug

- **6 of a suit other than trump** -- 1 or 3 key cards and failure to the named suit (this is only used if the suit of failure can be shown below the 6 level of the trump suit).

- **6 of the trump suit** --1 or 3 key cards and a failure in a suit of a higher level than the trump suit.

Finding the q of triumph

If the responder has 2 key cards, his chant of either ♥ ♠5 or 5 clarifies whether he has the trump q or not. You can also find out when the answer is 5♣ or 5♦.

To find out the initiator of the sequence rkcb, name 5 of the suit of the next step (5♦ on 5♣, 5 on 5).♦'

The two most common ways to answer:

1) The one who answers the question if he does not have the q of trump uses the first step. If he has the q of trump use the second step.

2) In this case the one who asks for the q claims to have the 5 key cards. The responder when he does not have the trump q says 5 of the trump suit. When he has it he names the cheapest side k he has.

If the initiator of the rkcb sequence, after you name your side k, names another suit, he is asking you if you have the k of that suit as well.

Here is an example:

a ♠9 4 3q 8 7 6   ♠

a ♥10 4   3k 5   ♥

♦ a 2   ♦ k 10 4 3

♣ 4 ♣ a j 5

opener:	responder:
12nt (forcing with)	♠
4nt (how many key cards?) 5	(I have 1 or 4 key cards.)
5♥ (do you have the one ♣ ?)	6 (I have it and also the k♦ but I don't have the k ♣.)
6♥ (you have the k♥.) 7	(got it)
pass (yay!)	

Looking for side kings

After the responses: 5♣ , 5 , 5 , 5 or 5♠ , the initiator of the rkcb sequence can use the chant of 5nt to ask the number of side kings held by responder. Since he has already shown or denied holding the trump k, he should not count it for his response.

The two most common ways to answer:

The one who asks about the kings, claims to have all the key cards and is showing interest in grand slam.

The two most common ways to answer are:

1) the steps are: 6♣ (no side kings), 6♦ (1 king), 6♥ (2 kings), ♠ (3 kings).

2) the steps are: 6♣ or 6♦ or   6o   6show the first k under the trump stick....

If you have extra strength or a source of tricks not yet shown (a solid side stick) you can accept by jumping to level 7.

Note:

There are many variations of the rkcb.

The "standard" responses are 5♣, 5♦, 5♥ and 5♠, and the rkcb initiator uses the cheapest club to ask for the trump q. Some pairs use different answers to show failures or the q answer.

Also answer number of side kings or name specific kings (instead of steps) when the rkcb initiator asks with 5nt.

Agree with your partner on these variations... to be sure you play the same.

CHAPTER VI. LETTER

1) With triumph

When the dead man's body is stretched, I go on to analyze the losers of the contract. If there are more than those required to fulfill the contract, I analyze which of the following variants I will execute to be able to fulfill it. Very important: I do not start the carding until I have decided the line of play.

1) elimination by purpose or expass
2) long stick affirmation (which will be the hand we have to affirm)
3) errors
4) discarding losers on side sticks with winning honors Theme 1 is the simplest, we will analyze it in practice.

Topic 2 is required:

a) good quality and quantity of wins, since it is usually necessary to first remove the opponent's wins.

b) sufficient entries in the hand that has the long pole to be able to enter when it is affirmed.

The 3rd theme: here we do not have to drag and we must have in one of the hands a long stick that must be short or miss in the other hand. It may happen that we have in both hands the possibility of failures, in this case it is called crossed failures.

Topic 4 will be discussed in practice.

These topics will be the ones we will be looking at in our first stage, as they are the most common and cover the largest number of hands.

2) Without triumph

We have to count winners, the missing ones can be obtained by few variants, what if other carding techniques appear.

1) They usually appear with the long suits of 5 cards or more, also of suits constructed with various honors -

2) For purposes

3) It is very important to keep all the clubs under control as much as possible (not to take immediate winning tricks until we generate our own tricks to fulfill the contract).

4) Delay a few shots in order to exhaust that stick on some of the opponents.

5) **Try to avoid the dangerous opponent (the one who has a signed stick and can run it).**

Exits

A)   Choice of the stick

1)   exit to stick mentioned by the partner

2)   stick out with consecutive honors ex.kqj42

3)   exit to unsung posts by the rivals

In s/t is added4   ) if I have other honors to my longer stick.

5)   if I have no short stick honors that can be important to my partner

6)   Avoid exits to clubs made up of e.g. a542 or j432 (any accompanying small cards).

B)   Once the suit has been chosen, the starting card must be chosen (we know that each card has a message for its partner). Let's show an example: the x's are small cards.

Akxxx-kqjx-j10 9 x with sequence of major

Qxxx - kxx with honor any length of the fourth or the smaller Xxxxx with white letters of the second.

This last one is only as a mention since it is a topic of many pages and very complex, that is why I suggest that if you want to improve in these two very important topics you should study some of the books on the subject. Without a doubt I recommend Francisco Pooper's book.

EPILOG

This moment is a great talk I have with you, I do not think I am able to expose thoughts that transcend, but I do believe I can give you life experiences that can be used by those who deem them important.

Everything refers to our brain, a muscle that for many is more important than the heart. And therefore, as we depend fundamentally on it to play bridge, I am giving it a whole chapter.

In my life I did everything, various business activities, sports of all kinds, some high performance, travel, I had a family, 4 children. During all that time, my body and physical activity had a lot of importance, of course my brain played its role.

At the age of 59 I had a car accident that changed my life, they thought I was dead, I was in intensive care for 3 months. There I began to realize that everything depended on me, I felt something that told me trust in you, you will overcome it.

At that time I felt incredible things, for example I had all my ribs broken, and they took me to surgery every 4 or 5 days because I had infected bones in one leg. The pain when they moved me is something that has no words, but I began to dominate it, there I realized that the brain had elements to use that were incredible, and I found in therapy that the ceiling became my TV and I began to pass movies of my life, I realized that if we send positive waves to the brain it solves most of the problems we have in our lives.

There I said: I had abandoned you for a long time and from now on I am going to dedicate myself to you because you are the one who is going to help me have a wonderful old age.

When I was 2 years old, they discovered a tumor in my head and they operated me, they took out the tumor and the whole left ear. I tell this story because I already went to that operation with the certainty that everything would be fine.

Let's wrap this up and go to the brain.
I realized that the most important thing for him was to have confidence in him, and to feed him I had to give him optimism, eliminate bad vibes, give him the least amount of problems.

He taught me that the most important thing was to love myself very much, but respecting others so as not to fall into selfishness, and I succeeded.

It taught me to enjoy the day as if it were the last day of my life, many people say I think the same, the question is: do you put it into practice or do you just know it?

This is the beginning of many of the things we know, but in practice we don't do. E.g. sports or exercises or daily walks rain or shine (I do them indoors). Listen to your body that warns you when something is wrong and go to the doctor to prevent it. And lastly, give your brain new challenges as often as possible, which is what it needs most to stay active. It can be anything: singing, dancing, studying languages, etc. .... or playing bridge.

Back to our book, this game was a fundamental factor in all this process that I had to live, and I think it is the one that helped me the most to be able to face and carry out those decisions and attitudes that I told you before. They say that several games are good to prevent brain diseases. I am going to list all the benefits of bridge and then you will decide if you want to learn it or not.

Bridge has an unparalleled number of virtues that are difficult to find to practice and maintain full mental activity.

I can divide them into two stages, youth and old age.

In the first, the most important is that it is an unparalleled source of logic application. We all say we want to be logical to get better results in our lives, but the hard part is how do we know and practice logical reasoning, bridge makes you practice it.

Another great advantage is that it is played as a team. Many sports are played as a team and we could say that this is enough, the difference is that bridge is a team of two, and the conjunction of these two minds is given by all the information that is transmitted during a hand, which are multiple and that each of the team members have to learn to listen. An issue that this time where the cell phone occupies most of our days, this virtue that is listening is very scarce. All this is to determine which contract should be played, but it does not end there, if we have to play against we also have information to pass and improve our game.

Finally, at this stage is that you play a different hand every 7 minutes, and no other game has that, that we have a new challenge so often. As I said in the book, in bridge as there is an unimaginable amount of hands, in all your playing life you can play a repeated hand.

As important things for old age, it constitutes a great challenge and an element to practice constancy and perseverance, things that are lost in old age. These attributes added to the above that we have explained, give us an important number of factors that will help people to have an active mind and prevent some of the risks that old age has for the brain.

Other very important issues for the elderly is that it allows us to socialize, as we can meet with friends to play or attend clubs where tournaments are played by many people, and allows us to talk with other players. There are also tournaments where you can travel, locally or internationally, including cruises where bridge is played.

As you can see this game is for everyone. In addition, as technology is coming so fast that soon we may have less time for work and more time for leisure, it will be difficult to fill useful spaces in our lives, bridge can be very useful.

You will say that I am very fond of bridge, but I really think that this and a few other things make this game important for our lives, and this book that facilitates the teaching in a considerable way can make many more people join to play it.

I am finishing one of the challenges of my life: writing a book I am sure it will be useful to you. See you next time.